Choir Of Day

New and Selected Poems

Cover image © 2011 by Edward F. Johnson

Published by

Ibebtson Street Press
25 School Street
Somerville MA 02143

ISBN: 978-0-9795313-3-0

Design by ISCSPress

Choir Of Day

New and Selected Poems

Robert K. Johnson

Ibbetson Street Press

Also by Robert K. Johnson

Poetry:

Blossoms Of The Apricot (1975)
The Wheel Of Daily Life (1988)
Four Poets, Four Voices (an anthology selection—1989)
Passing Moments (1992)
Out Of The Ordinary (1994)
City of Poets (an anthology selection—2000)
Sudden Turnings (2001)
The Latest News (2002)
From Mist To Shadow (2007)
Flowering Weeds (2008)

Nonfiction:

Francis Ford Coppola (1977)
Neil Simon (1983)

Acknowledgments

The new poems in this collection were originally published individually in the following magazines: *Abbey, The Aurorean, Free Verse, Iconoclast, Istanbul Literary Review, Main Channel Voices, Medusa's Kitchen, Minotaur, Pegasus, Poem, Poetry Porch, Presa, Purple Patch, Ripples, Sarasvati, Wilderness House Review,* and *Writers' Journal.*

For

Marc and Kate

Alone, aloud in the raptured ear of men
We pour our dark, nocturnal secret; and then,
    As night is withdrawn
From these sweet-springing meads and bursting boughs of May,
Dream, while the innumerable choir of day
    Welcome the dawn.

                    —Robert Bridges,"Nightingales"

Contents

New Poems

from *Blossoms Of The Apricot* (1975)

from *The Wheel Of Daily Life* (1988)

from *Four Poets, Four Voices* (1989)

from *Passing Moments* (1992)

from *Out Of The Ordinary* (1994)

from *City Of Poets* (2000)

from *Sudden Turnings* (2001)

from *The Latest News* (2002)

from *From Mist To Shadow* (2007)

from *Flowering Weeds* (2008)

New Poems

This Speck,

summer's last fly, protests
the year's first snow that covers
the trash can lid—won't settle there
but lifts its wisp of body
and circles in the darkening air.

And though, unlike the fly,
I have a mind and it tells me
"In vain," I—too—protest: despite
the chills of age, I keep
circling—in these straight lines I write.

On A Sunday Morning Sidewalk

On my way to buy onion bagels
and a paper from a store
open early, I see
a woman who walks, and pauses,

and walks in a minuet
with her busy poodle companion;
a young couple holding hands
inside a dream so warm

they don't know they're dressed too lightly
for such goosebumps-chilly air;
a trim man stoop to check
his bike's rear tire, then arc

his right leg over the seat,
push forward and whisper away.
And I feel so lucky to be
a note in this melody.

I Watch A Boy

not yet teen young
heave a basketball
toward his driveway's hoop,
and while the ball
lives out its arc
the boy wins and loses
his first love,

achieves diplomas
and marriage, plateaus
at his job, sees
the wonder of
his newborn son,
adores his daughter's
simplest acts

and—just as the ball
ends its flight—
he becomes a flame
of sadness
while watching a boy
heave a basketball
into endless time.

Linda: Fourteen

Loving you more than I do
everything else in the whole world,
loving you so much that it vibrates
like humming wire throughout my body,
throbs in my throat when I lie awake
at night, eats up all of me
day after day,

        I can't believe
when we're together at school, my love
never touches alive in you
the slightest stir of love for me,
never spurs you to even smile
at me. How is that possible?
It is not possible.

People I've Never Seen Before

walk into my midnight dreams,
thrust their hard jaw at me
and demand that I defend
some remark I made at noon,

or silently touch my lips
with the heat of their slow kiss,
or drive me to a dank cabin
deep in a woods I don't know.

How then can I deny
that despite the college degrees
I earned, the job-promotions
gained by my sweat and skills,

the upscale home I own—
despite everything I've achieved,
I am no more than a toy
for my dark mind to play with.

The First Time

After our first kiss ends
we open our eyes in a woods

where the sunlight slowly descends
steps made of ivy leaves,

and all the bark-bright trees
stand straight as palace guards

while clusters of branches swell
the air with their green silence,

and we, too, have no need for words.

The Journey
(for Séraphine de Senlis)

To gain the blaze-bright visions
she painted on canvases
she had to go farther and farther,

wherever the angel voices
that visited her mind
guided her. And she went

joyously, never demanding
a safe return.
                    Until,
when the last radiant painting

was finished, dried into beauty,
she had lost—as if it were
no more than a misplaced rag—

the way back to the grey town
where she long ago scrubbed floors;
while the voices hushed, and the gleaming

charged world they had helped her find
vanished, leaving her
locked in a silent limbo

with nothing
                    except what she,
having created it, owned
even after she died.

While Driving

home with the Sunday papers
I see Marc, our first-born,
now nine, pause on his bike
at the bottom of our hill
to check for cars. His feet
pressing down on the pedals;
his new headlight and horn—
all the accessories

he's lavished on his loved bike—
gleaming like his blond hair;
his shoulders squared and shawled
in sunlight:
               he stands full-length,
surprising me he's so tall.
And my brain and pumping blood—
every part of me says,
That's my son. My son.

Connections

We reach still another historic site
and from still another building nearby
comes the ceaseless din of hammers and drills;
and our street-tour guide suppresses a sigh

but can't help dropping his smile—and says,
"Noise follows me wherever I go."
And I think: with me, it's blunders I made
twenty, forty years ago.

Our Daughter's First Time Away From Home

You're so happy we came to see you
after your second week
at camp, when we start to drive

away, an impulse leads you
to discover what it feels like
to blow someone a kiss.

A Movie Scene

In *Casablanca*, always
when I saw Ilsa and Rick—
long after they parted in Paris—
meet in his restaurant
and feel in the same minute
the pain from the love they lost
and that same deep love reawaken,

I was sure—was positive—
that even though you and I
lived in the swarm of New York,
we would meet in a store or theater,
and time would slow, your face
turn ashen, and mine burn—

and while our breathing edged back
toward normal, we would talk—
ask questions so quietly
the people near where we stood
would never sense the tumult
underneath our words.

But the only thing
that happened concerning us
in all the years since we parted
happened today when I walked
to the busy street that housed
the firm where we had worked,
and found our building gone.

Open Heart Surgery

I came to consciousness
buried in a hospital bed,
three plastic containers attached
to my skin right under where
the incision had been made,
a two-pronged tube in my nose,
needles stuck in one arm,
my body—from head to foot—
too weak to even tremble;

while panic flung aside
my willpower's vow to be strong
as easily as a tornado
hurls rooftops miles away.
A scream—soundless, abject—
obliterated my brain.

    And although I, now, command
the direction my days' thoughts
and feelings take, I can't
forget I am someone who owns
a home that burglars stripped
of all his prize possessions
and who knows he can be robbed
again at any time.

A Goal

"Join us..." drawl my parents'
slightly drowsy friends,
a married couple who sit
in sunlight on the porch
my parents and I walk toward,
and who offer us slow smiles

peaceful as lullabies.
And in that moment, I learn
my goal in life: to be
someone just like these two
sprawled on a porch swing
in their casual clothes—so relaxed

they seem boneless as beach towels—
the Sunday papers spread
haphazardly in their laps—
their coffee cups half-full—
one buttered bagel left
on the plate. So I smile back,

happy for them and happy
to know my goal will be
so easy to reach,
                        although
decades have come and gone
and I still have not attained it.

Early April

All of March
was snow or sleet
or a sky-wide blotch
of cloud, grey
as a dirty bed sheet.
            But today
the clear sky fills
the quivering air
with a silver sheen;
tossed by the breeze
the still-bare
branches of the trees
slide glistening rills
of silver along
their bobbing bark
while grass blades gleam
like the prongs
of polished forks—
            today
there is a silver song
            everywhere.

The Second Time

Like birdwings
rising into sunlight,
you're lifted till you hover
high in the trembling air.

Yet you still own the will
to steer your coming days
back down to the mapped earth.

But even though you remember
that first time's final pain,

you yield to your eyes' wish
and look again at her smile,
listen to the float
of its song, and say "Yessss"

　　　　　　—and begin
that irreversible flight
to a place you know you don't know.

Just Like

other people, they rise
and wash their still-yawning face,
sip bracing coffee, and drive

through impeded traffic to work,
drive home to a hello
from their spouse and a quiet dinner,

and then bed, perhaps to make
tender love—
              all this because

their daily medication
is a cage that keeps behind bars
the pacing panther of madness.

Joie De Vivre

When drugs won't keep at bay
the ever-crueler pain
pulling my life away

from the bedroom curtains' lace,
the taste of succulent food,
even the tear-wet face

of my wife holding my hand—
when hot pain starts to pull me
into the dark's endless land,

I hope I can still tip
my head to the left or right
and kiss the cool pillowslip.

A Breakthrough

Breaking my right wrist—
the wrist I've lived by lo
these many years—has brought me
pain, hours of exasperation

during an E.R. wait,
a heavy cast that renders
my wrist helpless for five weeks,
plus one good thing.
                    I had been—

amid increasing unease—
aware that my days were kept
on an ever-shorter leash
of habits, that everything

in the world I saw was quickly
scissor-cut to fit
my encrusted point of view.
But propelled by my fall on the ice,

I'm forced to discover the still-
uncultivated land
of my left hand and help it
improve its skill in shaving

the bristles off my face,
in steering a fork to my mouth.
Even better, I've had to learn
to think left-handedly.

My Memory Is No Longer

a loyal lackey
ready to respond

to my command,
but a capricious flirt

who might, if I ask,
cuddle close to me,

but is just as likely
to flit—laughing—from the room,

then reappear
an hour or two later

and, if in the mood,
whisper in my ear

the name or date
I'm still trying to remember.

Remembering My Father

Despite the colliding jealousies,
the long barrages of angry shouts,
the resentments that never drifted away,
   your hopes that you could bring peace to our home
kept you calm, let you live your daily routines—

take Timmy, our white spitz, for strolls,
read five or six chapters from the Bible,
listen to your favorite radio shows.
   But, finally, you could no longer
not see that the rivalries and feuds,

the tempers quick to erupt still again
got worse, tore our family apart—
till your hopes plummeted like birdwings
ripped to shreds by a hunter's bullets.
   And, tinder dry, the deep despair

those daily routines had rendered harmless
ignited like a white-hot fire
engulfing a house's walls and roof;
and none of my desperate pleas could stop you
from walking into those roasting flames.

If You Die First
(for Pat)

will I wake up at midnight sobbing
face-down into my black pillow?

or, up at sunrise, prod my body
through daylong chores in the hope

I keep from exploding into fragments?
or attend a social mixer, chat

with a dozen women all strangers to me
while I try to convince myself

what's taking place is real?
               —I have no idea
what I will do if you die first.

Coda

The sky above these roofs
right to its farthest edges

is glistening blue
                    while a plane

soundlessly pulls its silver
still higher; the tree's thin limbs,

leafless as harp strings,
barely offer a stir

when the sunlit air remembers
to unroll a moment's breeze;

my curtains loll motionless
as Southern weeping willows;

and I, empty now of all
regrets and long-nursed hurts,

feel a joy so calm
it is almost not even joy.

from *Blossoms Of The Apricot* (1975)

Travelers

Inside my brain;
tangled in blankets
long since rubbed bald
of woolen down;
wearing bruised clothes:

the Don
          and Sancho
clumsily sleep....
Till the dawn-wind scuffs
their skin. Then, slowly,

on legs the cold
stiffened to stilts,
they rise, teeter
in the bleary air;
scratch. Then saddle

and mount the remains
of their horse, their donkey
and, still wordless,
resume
the usual pace.

While I, in my room,
no longer reading
the book, nor watching
the smoke from my cigarette
thaw into air,

I—not thin, not fat,
yet lean as the one,
paunchy as the other—
I doggedly follow
their bobbing backs.

Boyhood Creed

While kids, my friends and I
firmly believed that if you cut
  the rim of flesh that lies
between your forefinger and thumb,
  you—instantly—would die.

And, once, as someone passed
his new-bought knife around, one boy—
  grabbing too quickly—grasped
enough of the bare blade to nick
  that rim of flesh. We gasped.

Yet, when more than his share
of time went by and he still failed
  to suck vainly for air:
not joy, but angry bafflement
  replaced our mute despair.

Till he—trying to dim
the stares he faced—exclaimed: the blade
  must have *just missed* that rim.
We looked again and, soon, despite
  our eyes, agreed with him.

Men In City Parks

It is their stolidness
that I admire...
                    those men
who lumber to a halt
in sun-hazed city parks,
lower their haunches into
the brittle grass, and sprawl,
slow as glaciers.

Buddhas in bulk,
                    they, slowly,
strip to the waist...
leaving their belts half-hidden
under the soft, white folds
of their sagging stomachs.

                    Then, they gaze,
unblinking, blank-eyed, beyond
the grass that borders their flesh,
beyond the bobbing heads
of all the passersby;
                    wholly absorbed
in their own thoughts, remote
as a trail of clouds
hung in a windless sky....

To My Father

Now that you are dead,
all of our meetings match that time
I, after an evening in the City,
sat in Penn Station where I knew,
your night-shift ended, you too would come
to take the next train stopping at
our town.

Tired, staring at the haze
of smoke that dulled the ceiling lights
to a pale glare, I dozed off....
Then roused, not knowing where I was—
until I saw your smoke-grey form
standing a step in front of me.

As though you had expected us
to meet, your eyes showed no surprise.
Nor was there any need for me
to say, "I have been waiting for you."
All we did was gaze at each other,
silently.

Then you sat down
beside me. And we waited, together,
for the train that would take us home.

from *The Wheel Of Daily Life* (1988)

Lovers' Words

Each gliding gull that tips sunlight
across its tilting wings will die.
And so will love. Warm as those wings,
my love for you will die the day
I die.
 Why then, you ask, is it
not just as possible that time
will kill my love before I die?
before this year—this spring day—ends?
What have the moments when we kiss
and feel a slowly cresting warmth
fill our flesh or when we tell
each other truths about ourselves
never revealed before—what have
even these moments bred or fostered
that is not as helpless as your flesh
when you awake during the night
gripped by the fear that, come morning,
the love we share will be as dead
as flowers frozen by an early frost?
 You ask...and all my answers prove
I do not know.

White Rose Petals

The moment
   you realize

   the rose's
rings of petals

are
   open mouths

   white
with ecstasy

you will also
   discover

   your pores
are open mouths

white
   with ecstasy

from *Four Poets, Four Voices* (1989)

College Teaching

To teach is to stand
on the island—bare
except for a desk—
at the front of a classroom
and put your ideas
inside bottles of
clear sentences
and push each bottle—
by means of your voice—
toward the blank sea
of faces that lies
before your eyes.
—That's on a good day.
    On other days,
to teach is to poke
a huge, dry sponge.

My View Of A New England Autumn

Unlike this autumn, dying
a few leaves at a time,
my father waved back to me
as I left his hospital room;
and, a minute later, gasped
in pain and died.
                    Nor did my mother,
in her last month, become
more beautiful every day.
Her grey hair thinned,
revealing a flaking scalp.
Her cheeks puffed up
like a big doll's cheeks. Then,
while I bent over her bed,
her eyes hardened
like blue water turning to ice.

from *Passing Moments* (1992)

Mountain Stream

At noon on a bridge
in high country
    I stare at
a stream crammed
with bursting water
mad with speed and
cracking into foam
caromed off
both banks and hurled
past humps of rock
right below where I stand
stunned to see
inside myself.

Barbara: To Her Husband

When I take the backroads home on winter days
I have to remember there is a spot that stays
iced over even after the sun's rays
have melted all the other ice. And always
while driving over this spot, I remember, too:
exactly the same thing is true of you.

The Lecture

You lecture well in class. You clarify
the poem's compressed syntax, paraphrase
the wording in each stanza, pinpoint why
the form supports the content, cite the ways
the central meaning echoes what we know
were the most popular beliefs the year
the poem was written, and, concluding, show
how those beliefs touch our lives.—Then you hear
the end-of bell and watch your students spring
to their feet, grab their hats and coats, and flee
the classroom. And, glancing outside, you see
the sunlight splash a swooping bluejay's wings
gold-bright...and know no word your students heard
roused what, in you, that flash of sunlight stirred.

from *Out Of The Ordinary* (1994)

My Goal

is to write a poem whose form
disappears in the content
like sugar in hot coffee;
and whose content rivets the reader
the way footsteps in the next room
grip someone who had thought
he was in the house alone.

Waterfall

To see
a waterfall's
ton-heavy water
frozen motionless

and to know
it will remain
suspended until
the spring sun releases it

is to learn
how a poet can write
long afterwards
of taut moments in his life.

Food For Thought

The pigeons that
three months ago
      I saw
balancing their
unruffled feathers
      on a beam
of a warehouse
half torn down
      today
at the same place
are making themselves
      at home
on a beam of a half-
finished apartment
      house.

Suddenly, To My Wife

Unlike you,
who skirt our couch's chipped legs
with frills and then forget
even the frills, my brain
still sees those legs, and the dust
buried under our rugs.

When we visit
your aunt in the hospital
you remove the vase's dead flowers
and arrange a fresh bouquet;
while the shadows under her eyes
suck my breath away.

And I know
that what you do is right,
is the only way to act
when trapped in a body
concealing a bomb that may not
explode for months, for years.

And I know
the hate I feel for you
when I watch you do these things
is wrong, and natural
as the rage a cripple feels
watching someone walk.

Jephthah

I keep remembering when
those strangers, my half-brothers,
led the elders to
my hideout and offered me—
bastard and outlaw—the rule
of their land if I freed it
from the threat of foreign rule.
Even the table and chairs
seemed astonished. I,
cast out by my brothers,
would be their king.
                    My soft
"Yes," heavy with hatred,
sounded humble.

               That night,
on bended knee, I bartered:
If granted victory,
I would surrender to
our loving Lord
the first who—saved from death
by my triumph—came from my house
to greet me.

             I never thought
it would be she.

             I knew
it would be she; for that
was what increased the chance
my vow would be found worthy....

When I returned from the righteous
slaughter of our heathen foes:
she, my daughter,
my only child, lifting
her timbrels above her head,
danced toward me.

There was no need to tell her
the details of what would happen;
she envisioned them
as she stood staring at me.
The veins in her white neck
throbbed. I wanted to touch
those veins with my fingers;
but I could not move my hand.
Or speak. Or look away....

Untied, but held, I watched
while my daughter, surrounded by
tree roots and branches,
felt the rising flames
free her from the tight ropes....

She is dead, yet relentless.
For the sandals I wear are those
she brought me every morning.
I still trim my beard
to the length she liked best.
The evening wine I sip
is the color of her lips.

Somehow, whether in sunlight
or in shadow, the simplest flower
outwits me.

        I sacrificed
my loving daughter
whom I loved—but did
not know I loved so much—
in order to rule over
my brothers, whom I hate
because they never loved me.
I, a raging man
who brought his people peace....

from *City Of Poets* (2000)

Smacked

onto the asphalt
by a speeding tire,

the squirrel—
trying to stand up—

jerks less and
less—until

the twitches
that its tail makes

are explained
only by the wind.

A Morning To Remember

The summer breeze that brings
the kitchen curtains to life
as it floats through my window

also brings the high-pitched
"Hellooo" of Jimmy Morley
who, when I first look outside,

holds up his ball and mitt—
ready to play catch—
the week before he drowned.

In Any Piece Of Music

it is always
a sequence

shorter
than ten notes

that holds my breath
still as sunlight

and tells me
not to describe

a poem's
delivery-room setting

or even
the baby's wet birth

but solely
the baby's

first red cry.

Out In The Suburbs

Every kind of finch
sits nicely on your feeder;

robins and blue jays
complement your lawn.

A crow does neither.
Nor does it hop-hop-hop

like a melody in motion
toward your azaleas.

It lumbers side to side—
like a short linebacker—

across your picnic table
until its tracks render the top

unfit for food. Then it rises
on wings that bully their way

through the air; and sags a branch
right above your roof

while it decides what to do
with the last meal it digested.

from *Sudden Turnings* (2001)

Almost A Dance

Sitting close to him
at a café's outdoor table,
she describes in bursts of words

some wonderful film she saw
or scenic drive she took,
while the morning's faint breeze

nudges the tips of her hair.
Once and then again
she raises her right arm

as if she were tossing her words—
like tiny flower petals—
high into the sunlight.

                He leans
still nearer to her chair
to block out everything

that isn't her, and his eyes
express a delight so palpable
it ripples through the air

like rapid trumpet notes—
a delight so all-consuming
it consumes even me,
just strolling by.

For One Afternoon

After so many years,
I have forgotten her last name
or where on the West Side she lived.
I remember only what I felt
on that mid-winter Sunday when,
out late the night before
and now together again,
we finished our toast and tea
and settled deep into a couch
that a rim of sunlight barely reached.

Sometimes we kissed. Or finger-traced
each other's face. Or drifted
in and out of the fog of sleep.
And all the while, we half-listened
to a cellist in the next apartment
practice a piece that neither of us knew,
listened for an hour, two hours
while the cellist played
and replayed passages
as slowly as the shifting sunlight
covered us with its weightless gold.

The High For Me As A Teacher

is to devise
a lecture that soon

lures the students
who tilted

their back-row chairs
against the wall

into leaning
so far forward

to better hear
what I say next

they bring
those chairs' front legs

back down
to the floor.

Strolling Up

Fifth Avenue,
we were red-lighted
to a pause

that you used
to give me
a quick kiss.

"What?"
I said, "what was that
about?"

Looking
at some blue companion
in the sky,

you replied,
"I'll never tell!"
—And because you

never did,
that moment's warmth
is still on my lips.

What I Hear

The way my wife,
     in another room,

once said to me,
     "Bob—come quick,"

in a tone that wiped out
     any thought

of my replying,
     "Not now—later,"

is the way the world
     I wake to

calls to me
     every day.

A Thief

Like a midnight burglar
who finds the one

open window
or unlocked door

and swiftly slips
inside the house:

what you worried most
about all day

seizes the one moment
when you half-rouse

during the night
and steals your sleep.

After All These Years

I find my life
's goal
defined

when I see
a girl break
away from strolling

friends, clasp
a street sign
's pole

with her out-
stretched hand
and whirl

around
and around
while one strand

of her hair,
faint
as a rope's shadow

on a sail,
slants
across her cheek.

from *The Latest News* (2002)

Out There

Standing across from the State House
every day, you flick

a small American flag
as if it were a whip

and shout venom about homosexuals,
millionaire athletes, meter maids,

dog owners, foreign cars,
cancer-causing Asian food.

Lean and hot as hate,
you need no hat or coat

while the words from your blue-veined lips
harangue the air

or the startled drivers paused
at the light or walkers who quickly

veer away from you. I, too,
always hurry by—

but silently offer you my thanks
for reminding me

even our daily world's sunniest noon
includes not only

cars whose engines won't start
and computers down for a day,

but madness.

The Latest News

Another man runs amok,
murders a mix of strangers
sunbathing in a city park—

and before the blood has dried,
another expert is on camera
telling his tv audience

the killer could and therefore should
have been detected
and given therapy till rendered

no threat to society.
Then viewers blank their screens
and sleep the sleep of the reassured.

And never allow themselves to think
that, though skilled when it comes
to spotting flaws in a movie plot

or errors in a restaurant check,
they will always fail to perceive
that a man boyscout-polite

when met on the apartment stairs
may chuckle in his midnight bed
remembering the childhood day

his knife, for the first time,
dissected a writhing cat;
will always fail to confront the fact

that urges brutal and reverseless
as a bullet in mid-flight
can rage in someone's blood

from the dawn he first sucks milk
right to the sunny afternoon
he pulls out his mad gun

and splatters a park's green grass
with the blood of a dozen strangers
taken completely by surprise.

from *From Mist To Shadow* (2007)

Snow-Portrayed

Snowflakes that fall
so thick and fast
they overwhelm the air

and pelt our bodies
with swarms of whiteness
until we gasp

are snowflakes
that describe joy.
          Describing

happiness
are snowflakes
that scatter downward

steadily but
so lightly they fail
to hold our attention

when we leave the house.
Nor do they hamper
traffic or chill

our feet as we walk
from store to store
through their thin sprinkle.

Only near day's end
as we trudge
toward our front door,

         only then
do we see—
with such surprise

it slows our breath—
that these casual flakes
melted all the sidewalks,

shrubs and lawns
to a bright glow
we, now, stop to savor.

The Definitive NYC Story
(from *The New York Times*)

The first of the two girls
walking toward their private school
asks, "So how was your weekend?"

"Terrible," the second girl replies.
"My mother had a nervous breakdown
right on Fifth Avenue."

                    "Wow!"
the first girl says. "Fifth and what?"

Dusk Shadows On Jones Beach
(for Alice P.)

More than being glad when I say that you
are right—the rows of darkening waves
haven't chilled my bare skin blue,

more than your pleasure when I erase,
with my towel's caressing strokes, the drops
of ocean on your tanned face

is the sadness that won't let you forget
whose kiss, like soft fire, warmed your lips
on this beach before we met.

Saturdays With My Mother

Every dusk,
when my footsteps reached
the car, I turned
and, always,

even if all day long
she was hard to please,
quick to quarrel,

she stood—her eyes
riveted on me,
her puffy cheeks
sagged to stillness—

in front of the dark door
she would soon
have to enter

—until the day
the strokes began
and, months later,
ended.

       Now,
each time I see her
she is standing,

waiting in the dusk
that darkens
only me
to sadness.

In Front Of The 42nd Street Library

My wife and I wait near the curb,
but my eyes roam the library's park
and stop at the time-greyed bench
where a woman and I once sat at dusk

while the hurrying traffic's noise
was soon stilled—smothered by
the weight of our whispered words.

She listened to my impassioned plea.
I spurned the stubborn sense
her parched lips managed to phrase.

Then we stared at the chill air
a few unendurable minutes
until, in order to breathe, we stood up,

heard—almost in disbelief—
our voices say, "Goodbye,"
and walked into opposite darknesses.

Now a cab pulls up at the curb
and I open the door for my smiling wife,
get in beside her and begin
to write this poem.

Last Night
(October 18, 2001)

I saw a movie made
three or four years ago
that deftly used two hours

for a story that portrayed
life in a city school,
but a story pale in its powers

compared to the truth conveyed
in the film's split-second view
of what was once the Twin Towers.

Matins

The dawn's first hints of light
are faint as piano notes
played by tentative fingers.

Although my patio's cement
insists on its stillness,
thin tufts of mist curl upwards
like white whispers.

Roused from sleep,
the ivy-housed sparrows
cheep their excitement into an air

that slowly swells from grey
to a blazing gold
that glistens in the narrow grooves
of my oak trees' bark.

Grass blades rise up shining
while bushes let the light
flow through their clusters of green.

Even the dark needles
that lie beneath
the lowest pine tree branches
glow a brighter black.

And so, the stir of another dawn
urges me to love
all the hours still to come.

At Sunrise

The first thing our still sleepy eyes
see in the dawnlit breakfast nook
is the mess. Cookbooks knocked askew
across the bottom shelf; a plant
that landed far from its toppled stand,
its potted dirt now a path on the floor;
a wastebasket's contents strewn everywhere.

Then, of course, we see the squirrel
crouched in a corner, twitching its tail
in readiness. We try to shoo it
toward the door, but it runs the other way.
When we push it with our broom, it attacks—
rips out the straw and leaps at our hands.

We win a kitchen restored to order
only after an hour's battle—
after a favorite lamp lies shattered
and we at last have managed to trap
the squirrel in a neighbor's fishnet

and toss its thrashing, panting body
out on our backyard patio
where, at sunset, we like to sit
and enjoy our view of nature.

A Manhattan Moment

I can tell you
that the yellow turned
to red and I stepped
off the curb

and a car
passed inches
from my front shoe
so bullet-fast

I can't tell you
about panic
or rage, sorrow
or regret.

All I felt
a minute later
was open-mouthed
amazement—

to be already
thinking about
what to have
for lunch.

Seen On A Midnight Walk

A part of each of us,
asleep or awake,
is these five mallards

hidden from sight
all night long
unless for one moment

they happen to cross
the dream-like streak
of shimmering silver

a streetlight casts
on the pond's
rippleless water—

five curved shapes,
always silent, always
floating in the dark.

Lying Beneath A Maple Tree
   (For Pat)

Thirteen, I was pulled so deep
    into the countless shades of green
found in the sun-hazed leaves,
    I wanted this lush sight to mean

even more than its bountiful self.
    And it did. When we first met, I knew—
in one breath—those glistening leaves
    were a foreshadowing of you.

A Reunion
As If At Grand Central Station

Standing in front
of the information booth

Life—
more beautiful than ever—

begins to smile
as only she can smile

the moment I appear in view
after enduring a week

worse than being locked
in solitary confinement

while I waited
for the results of the lab test.

Now, walking faster and faster,
I scatter the air in my path

      until at last
Life and I hug rib-tight,

then laugh—
laugh right up to the rafters.

Returning A Year Later

The shining headstone
over young Billy's grave
is a lie. The bright green mound

—another lie. The cemetery's
miles of morning sunlight
—lies, all lies.

Only the dark stain
on the lingering moon
tells the truth.

Pavane

At the end
of the long corridor's

bewilderment of sudden turns
past rooms filled with furniture

strangers put in place,
past rooms with picture-framed faces

that resemble people you once knew,
and then rooms depleted of everything

but walls grey as old stones,
you will find yourself

standing in a gold-bright air
as alive as your quickened pores

and you will see a distant bird
gliding with sunlight on its wings

across a shining field
where the tip of a tree's low branch

waits for the bird to alight.
                    And you will know.

from *Flowering Weeds* (2008)

Again In May

Day after late-spring day,
from my oak trees' lowest limbs
to the tips of their top branches,
swarms of caterpillars

eat the leaves' green spans
with so much passion that I,
almost asleep, can hear them
in the darkness. And my greed

matches their hungry mouths.
I want to taste every food
and wine, book and film,
mountain, city, ocean—

devour everything displayed
on the long buffet of riches
the dawn light offers me
day after day all year.

To Be Sixteen

is to hear—
a block away

from your school's
football field—

the bassdrum beat
of the band, the wind-

lifted cheers
of your classmates

and to hurry your feet
into a run

so that the rising
roar

inside you
can join

what waits
just up ahead.

A Personal Preference

    Yes I, too,
like to see
a butterfly

that after a rest
from flight,
unfolds its wings

    and makes
a moment's
parasol

for the flower
beneath its wisp
of weight

    —but, more,
I love to watch
a bull-chested crow

    plop
its black fat
on a thin limb

that instantly bends,
as if begging
for mercy.

Karen

Your hair still all wrong,
the food stains on your blouse
another reason your male classmates
never ask you for a date,
though I would, if I could,

and the latest poetry you write
even more delicate and intense
than the first poems, four years ago,
your head-down whisper asked me
to read if I had the time:

now, about to graduate,
you breathlessly detail to me
your plan to head for the Northwest
because you've heard there's land out there
that's still unspoiled, still pristine.

And although I'm able to lecture for hours
on *Oedipus Rex* and *Moby Dick*,
I can't think of a way to tell you
that what you really want out west
does not exist anywhere.

Brute Beauty

Now the landscape is wiped clean
of all the huddled bushes'
timid bits of greenery,
all eager-to-please rose petals

and witless butterfly flutters,
the dull droop of clustered leaves
and incessant flittings of flies.
        Now, under the grey glare

of the heavy sky, the landscape stands
stripped to seriousness,
marked only by the stretch
of its stark branches, grass blades

juiceless as straw, and brick-hard dirt—
a landscape primed to receive
the merciless white passion
of a snowstorm's pelting flakes.

When Embattled

To know your mind consists
of a castle with parapets,
and that if part of the bulwark
cannot withstand the pressures

that besiege your days, you can always
rally your reasoning powers
and, sharp as a sword, repulse
your enemy
                    is to live

in a child's fairyland.
Your mind is no stalwart fortress
but a flag high on a pole
in an outpost, and someday

rampaging doubts and fears
you can't even imagine now
will rear up, primal and wild,
rip that flag to shreds
and hurl it into darkness.

Inside A Church In Rome

Even the day I waited
for a life-or-death lab report,
I accepted the sky as empty

of everything but clouds,
and the grave as the dark home
of nothing except decay;

but now, in the dim light
of this church, my tourist eyes
see right in front of me

a white-haired woman, thin
as a candle flame,
kneeling at the altar rail,

wholly absorbed in the prayer
her lips silently recite—
and I'm wrapped inside the swirl

of a measureless longing
to share the faith that feeds
this woman's life. A breath later

I feel miles away from her
and from the gust of longing
that shook me a moment ago.

Older

You listen to a concert's
swirls of melody
or to the silent hum
of sunlight on your face

and what rises deep inside you
like a surge of june-warm surf
climbing a sand dune's slope

is a new nameless feeling
that, somehow, includes

the press of love,
the dogged grip of regret,
catapulting joy
and even merciless pain

and leads you to accept,
as calmly as willow leaves
accept a stir of wind,

everything past and present
in your unfathomable life.

Robert K. Johnson, after earning graduate degrees at Cornell University and Denver University, was a Professor of English and Creative Writing for many years, including at Suffolk University. Upon retiring, he became, first, Submissions Editor and then Consulting Editor for *Ibbetson Street* magazine. Many of his poems have appeared individually in a variety of magazines and newspapers. Eight collections of his poetry have been published, the most recent being *From Mist To Shadow* and *Flowering Weeds*.

www.ingramcontent.com/pod-product-compliance
Lightning Source LLC
La Vergne TN
LVHW091310080426
835510LV00007B/448